100 facts on Dinosaurs

100 facts on
Dinosaurs

Steve Parker

Consultant: Dr Jim Flegg

BARDFIELD
PRESS

First published by Bardfield Press in 2006
Copyright © Miles Kelly Publishing Ltd 2001

This edition published in 2007 by Bardfield Press

Bardfield Press is an imprint of
Miles Kelly Publishing Ltd
Bardfield Centre, Great Bardfield, Essex, CM7 4SL

This material was first published as hardback in 2001
and as flexiback in 2004 by Miles Kelly Publishing Ltd

2 4 6 8 10 9 7 5 3

Editorial Director: Belinda Gallagher
Art Director: Jo Brewer
Assistant Editor: Lucy Dowling
Volume Designer: Sally Lace
Picture Researcher: Liberty Newton
Proofreader/Indexer: Jane Parker
Reprographics: Anthony Cambray, Liberty Newton
Production Manager: Elizabeth Brunwin

ISBN 978-1-84236-768-1

Printed in China

British Library Cataloguing-in-Publication Data
A catalogue record for this book is available from the British Library

ACKNOWLEDGEMENTS
The publishers would like to thank the following artists who have contributed to this book:

Chris Buzer/Studio Galante, Jim Channell, Flammetta Dogi/Scientific Illust.,
Chris Forsey, Mike Foster/Maltings Partnership, L R Galante/Studio Galante,
Brooks Hagan/Studio Galante, Alan Hancocks, Stuart Lafford/Linden Artists Ltd,
Kevin Maddison, Alan Male/Linden Artists, Janos Marffy, Alessandro Menchi/Studio Galante,
Massimiliano Maugeri/Studio Galante, Francesco Spadoni/Studio Galante, Rudi Vizi,
Steve Weston/Linden Artists, Mike White/Temple Rogers

Cartoons by Mark Davis at Mackerel

www.mileskelly.net
info@mileskelly.net

Contents

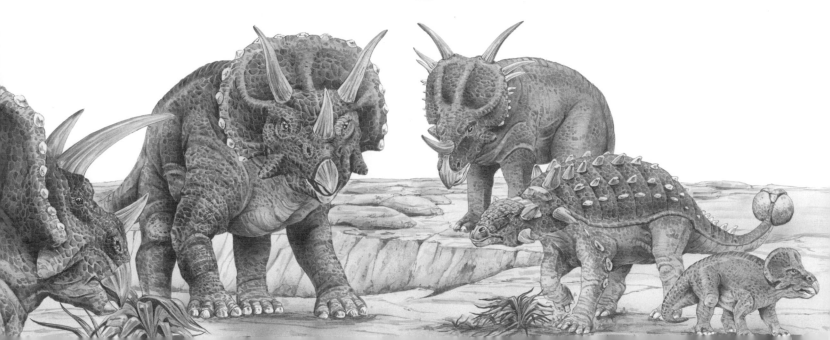

World of the dinosaurs

1 Dinosaurs were types of animals with scaly skin, called reptiles. They lived millions of years ago. There were many different kinds of dinosaurs – huge and tiny, tall and short, fierce hunters and peaceful plant-eaters. But all the dinosaurs died out long, long ago.

Age of the dinosaurs

2 Dinosaurs lived between about 230 million and 65 million years ago. This vast length of time is called the Mesozoic Era. Dinosaurs were around for about 80 times longer than people have been on Earth!

This timeline begins 286 million years ago at the start of the Permian Period when the ancestors of the dinosaurs appear. It finishes at the end of the Tertiary Period 2 million years ago, when the dinosaurs die out and mammals became dominant.

3 Dinosaurs were not the only animals during the Mesozoic Era. There were many other kinds of such as insects, fish, scurrying lizards, crocodiles, feathered birds and furry mammals.

4 There were many different shapes and sizes of dinosaurs. Some were smaller than your hand. Others were bigger than a house!

Jobaria and Janenschia, giant plant-eaters.

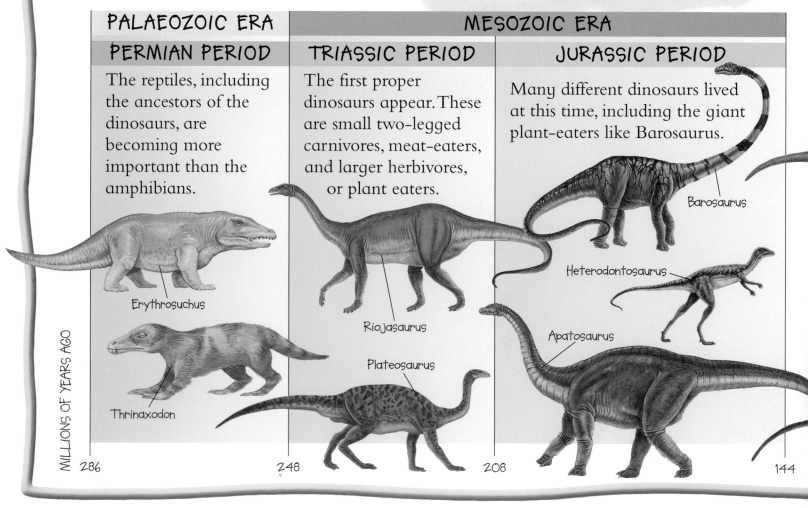

PALAEOZOIC ERA	MESOZOIC ERA	
PERMIAN PERIOD	TRIASSIC PERIOD	JURASSIC PERIOD
The reptiles, including the ancestors of the dinosaurs, are becoming more important than the amphibians.	The first proper dinosaurs appear. These are small two-legged carnivores, meat-eaters, and larger herbivores, or plant eaters.	Many different dinosaurs lived at this time, including the giant plant-eaters like Barosaurus.

Erythrosuchus

Thrinaxodon

Riojasaurus

Plateosaurus

Barosaurus

Heterodontosaurus

Apatosaurus

MILLIONS OF YEARS AGO

286

248

208

144

5 **No single kind of dinosaur survived for all of the Mesozoic Era.** Different kinds came and went. Some lasted for less than a million years. Other kinds, like Stegosaurus, kept going for more than 20 million years.

6 **There were no people during the Age of Dinosaurs.** There was a gap of more than 60 million years between the last dinosaurs and the first people.

I DON'T BELIEVE IT!

The name 'dinosaur' means 'terrible lizard'. But dinosaurs weren't lizards, and not all dinosaurs were terrible. Small plant-eating dinosaurs were about as 'terrible' as today's sheep!

◄ All the dinosaurs died out at the end of the Cretaceous Period, possibly because of a meteor strike, but no one can be sure.

MESOZOIC ERA	CENOZOIC ERA
CRETACEOUS PERIOD	TERTIARY PERIOD
During the last part of the age of the dinosaurs, both giant carnivores and armoured herbivores were alive.	The dinosaurs have all died out. The mammals, that have been around since the Triassic Period, become the main land animals.

Tyrannosaurus rex

Deinonychus

Spinosaurus

Tarbosaurus

Brontotherium, herbivorous mammal

Thylacosmilus, carnivorous mammal

Nesodon, herbivorous mammal

144

65

2

MILLIONS OF YEARS AGO

Before the dinosaurs

7 **Dinosaurs were not the first animals on Earth.** Many other kinds of creatures lived before them, including many other types of reptiles. Over millions of years one of these groups of reptiles probably changed very slowly, or evolved, into the first dinosaurs.

9 **Some crocodiles look like dinosaurs – but they weren't.** Crocodiles were around even before the first dinosaurs. They still survive today, long after the last dinosaurs. Erythrosuchus was 4.5 metres long, lived 240 million years ago, lurked in swamps and ate fish.

8 **Dimetrodon was a fierce, meat– eating reptile that looked like a dinosaur – but it wasn't.** It lived 270 million years ago, well before the dinosaurs began. Dimetrodon was three metres long and had a tall flap of skin like a sail on its back.

10 Therapsids lived before the dinosaurs and also alongside the early dinosaurs. They were also called mammal-like reptiles because they didn't have scaly skin like most reptiles. They had furry or hairy skin like mammals.

Ornithosuchus was one of the early thecodonts. It was a carnivore that walked on two legs, a cousin of the first dinosaurs. The name 'thecodont' means 'socket-toothed reptile'.

QUIZ

1. Did Dimetrodon live before or after the dinosaurs?
2. Did thecodonts catch small animals to eat or munch on leaves and fruits?
3. What are therapsids also known as?
4. Did dinosaurs gradually change, or evolve into crocodiles?
5. Did all reptiles have scaly skin?

1. Before 2. Small animals 3. Mammal-like reptiles 4. No, crocodiles are separate. 5. No, some were furry

11 Thecodonts were slim, long legged reptiles which lived just before the dinosaurs. They could rear up and run fast on their back legs. They could also leap and jump well. They probably caught small animals such as bugs and lizards to eat.

12 Of all the creatures shown here, the thecodonts were most similar to the first dinosaurs. So perhaps some thecodonts gradually changed, or evolved, into early dinosaurs. This may have happened more than 220 million years ago. But no one is sure, and there are many other ideas about where the dinosaurs came from.

The dinosaurs arrive!

13 The earliest dinosaurs stalked the Earth almost 230 million years ago. They lived in what is now Argentina, in South America. They included Eoraptor and Herrerasaurus. Both were slim and fast creatures. They could stand almost upright and run on their two rear legs. Few other animals of the time could run upright like this, on legs that were straight below their bodies. Most other animals had legs which stuck out sideways and then bent down, and walked with a slow waddle.

Herrerasaurus was about 3 metres long from nose to tail.

The legs were underneath the body, not sticking out to the sides as in other reptiles such as lizards and crocodiles.

14 **These early dinosaurs were probably meat-eaters.** They hunted small animals such as lizards and other reptiles, insects and worms. They had lightweight bodies and long, strong legs to chase after prey. Their claws were long and sharp for grabbing victims. Their large mouths were filled with pointed teeth to tear up their food.

TWO LEGS GOOD!

You will need:

some stiff card safe scissors

sticky tape split pins

Cut out a model of Herrerasaurus; the head, body, arms and tail are one piece of card. Next, cut out each leg from another piece. Fix the legs on either side of the hip area of the body using a split pin. Adjust the angle of the head, body and tail to stand over the legs. This is how many dinosaurs stood and ran, well balanced over their rear legs and using little effort.

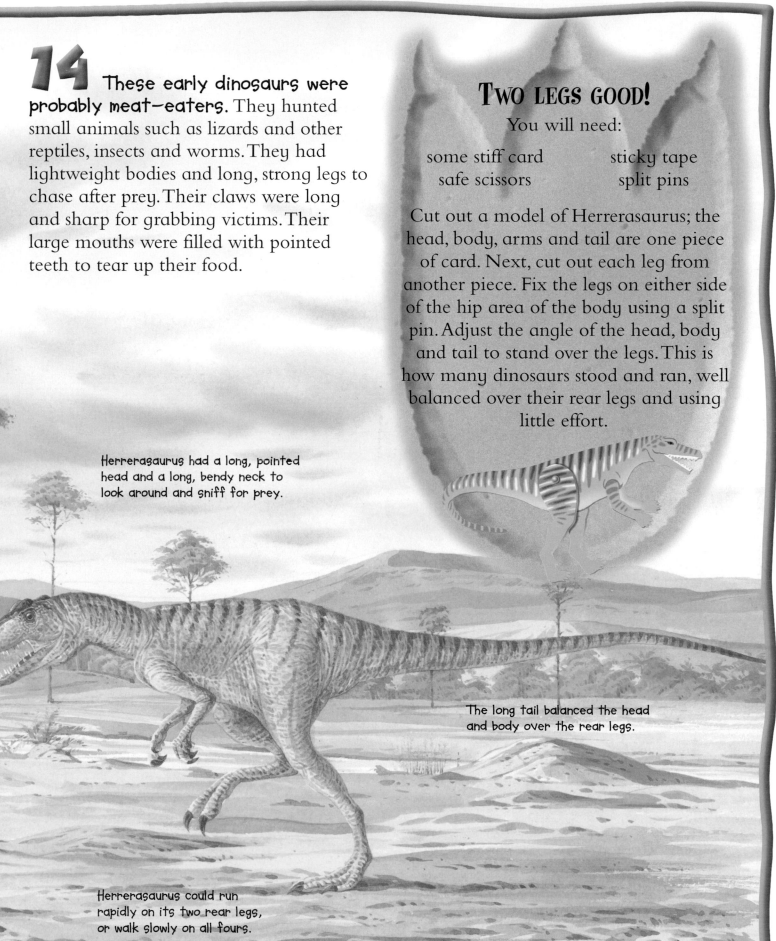

Herrerasaurus had a long, pointed head and a long, bendy neck to look around and sniff for prey.

The long tail balanced the head and body over the rear legs.

Herrerasaurus could run rapidly on its two rear legs, or walk slowly on all fours.

Getting bigger!

15 As the early dinosaurs spread over the land they began to change. This gradual and natural change in living things has happened since life began on Earth. New kinds of plants and animals appear, do well for a time, and then die out as yet more new kinds appear. The slow and gradual change of living things over time is called evolution.

▼ Plateosaurus

16 Some kinds of dinosaurs became larger and began to eat plants rather than animals. Plateosaurus was one of the first big plant-eating dinosaurs. It grew up to 8 metres long and lived 220 million years ago in what is now Europe. It could rear up on its back legs and use its long neck to reach food high off the ground.

17 Riojasaurus was an even larger plant-eater. It lived 218 million years ago in what is now Argentina. Riojasaurus was 10 metres long and weighed about one tonne – as much as a large family car of today.

▼ Riojasaurus

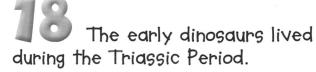

18 The early dinosaurs lived during the Triassic Period. This was the first period or part of the Age of Dinosaurs (the Mesozoic Era). The Triassic Period lasted from 248 to 208 million years ago.

19 The early plant-eating dinosaurs may have become larger so that they could reach up into trees for food. Their size would also have helped them fight enemies, as many big meat-eating reptiles were ready to make a meal of them. One was the crocodile Rutiodon which was 3 metres long.

▼ Rutiodon, a crocodile-like meat-eater, waits for Riojasaurus. It may be thinking about dinner!

I DON'T BELIEVE IT!

Early plant-eating dinosaurs did not eat fruits or grasses – there weren't any! They hadn't appeared yet! Instead they ate plants called horsetails, ferns, cycads, and conifer trees.

What teeth tell us

20 We know about living things from long ago, such as dinosaurs, because of fossils. These were once their hard body parts, such as bones, claws, horns and shells. The hard parts did not rot away after death but got buried and preserved for millions of years. Gradually they turned to stone and became fossils. Today, we dig up the fossils, and their sizes and shapes give us clues to how prehistoric animals lived.

▶ Plant-eater Edmontosaurus had flat teeth at the back of its jaws for chewing its food.

21 Dinosaur teeth were very hard and formed many fossils. Their shapes help to show what each type of dinosaur ate. Edmontosaurus had rows of broad, wide, sharp-ridged teeth in the sides of its mouth. These were ideal for chewing tough plant foods like twigs and old leaves.

▲ Tyrannosaurus had sharp, knife-like teeth at the front of its jaw for cutting and tearing meat.

22 Tarbosaurus had long, sharp teeth like knives or daggers. These were excellent for tearing up victims, and slicing off lumps of flesh for swallowing.

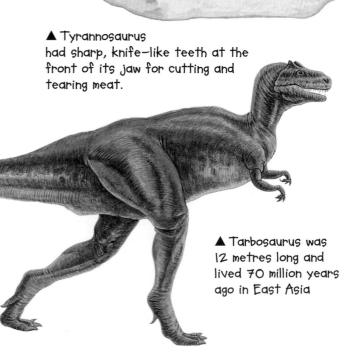

▲ Tarbosaurus was 12 metres long and lived 70 million years ago in East Asia

▼ Baryonyx was 10 metres long and lived 120 million years ago in Europe

FIND DINOSAUR TEETH AT HOME!

With the help of an adult, look in a utensils drawer or tool box for dinosaur teeth! Some tools resemble the teeth of some dinosaurs, and do similar jobs.

File or rasp – broad surface with hard ridges, like the plant-chewing teeth of Edmontosaurus.

Knife – long, pointed and sharp, like the meat-slicing teeth of Tyrannosaurus.

Pliers – Gripping and squeezing, like the beak-shaped mouth of Ornithomimus.

23 **Baryonyx had small, narrow, pointed, cone-shaped teeth.** These resemble the teeth of a crocodile or dolphin today. They are ideal for grabbing slippery prey such as fish.

24 **The teeth of the giant, long-necked dinosaur Apatosaurus were long, thin and blunt, shaped like pencils.** They worked like a rake to pull leaves off branches into the mouth, for the dinosaur to eat.

▶ Apatosaurus was 25 metres long and lived 140 million years ago in Western North America

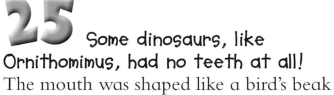

25 **Some dinosaurs, like Ornithomimus, had no teeth at all!** The mouth was shaped like a bird's beak and made out of a tough, strong, horny substance like our fingernails. The beak was suited to pecking up all kinds of food like seeds, worms and bugs, like birds do today.

▲ Ornithomimus was 3.5 metres long and lived 70 million years ago in western North America

Super-size dinosaurs

26 The true giants of the Age of Dinosaurs were the sauropods. These vast dinosaurs all had a small head, long neck, barrel-shaped body, long tapering tail and four pillar-like legs. The biggest sauropods included Brachiosaurus, Mamenchisaurus, Barosaurus, Diplodocus and Argentinosaurus.

▲ Argentinosaurus was up to 40 metres long, and weighed up to 100 tonnes.

27 Sauropod dinosaurs probably lived in groups or herds. We know this from their footprints, which have been preserved as fossils. Each foot left a print as large as a chair seat. Hundreds of footprints together showed many sauropods walked along with each other.

28 Sauropod dinosaurs may have swallowed pebbles — on purpose! Their peg-like teeth could only rake in plant food, not chew it. Pebbles and stones gulped into the stomach helped to grind and crush the food. These pebbles, smooth and polished by the grinding, have been found with the fossil bones of sauropods.

29 The biggest sauropods like Apatosaurus were enormous beasts. They weighed up to ten times more than elephants of today. Yet their fossil footprints showed they could run quite fast – nearly as quickly as you!

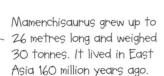

Mamenchisaurus grew up to 26 metres long and weighed 30 tonnes. It lived in East Asia 160 million years ago.

Barosaurus lived 150 million years ago in North America and Africa. It was 27 metres long and weighed 15 tonnes.

Brachiosaurus grew up to 25 metres long, and weighed up to 50 tonnes. It lived 150 million years ago in North America and Africa.

Diplodocus lived in North America 150 million years ago. It grew to 27m long and weighed up to 12 tonnes.

30 Sauropods probably had to eat most of the time, 20 hours out of every 24. They had enormous bodies which would need great amounts of food, but only small mouths to gather the food.

This modern lorry is to the same scale as these huge dinosaurs!

I DON'T BELIEVE IT!

Diplodocus is also known as 'Old Whip-tail'! It could swish its long tail so hard and fast that it made an enormous CRACK like a whip. This living, leathery, scaly whip would scare away enemies or even rip off their skin.

Claws for killing

31 Nearly all dinosaurs had claws on their fingers and toes. These claws were shaped for different jobs in different dinosaurs. They were made from a tough substance called keratin - the same as your fingernails and toenails.

32 Hypsilophodon had strong, sturdy claws. This small plant-eater, 2 metres long, probably used them to scrabble and dig in soil for seeds and roots.

33 Deinonychus had long, sharp, hooked claws on its hands. This meat-eater, about 3 metres long, would grab a victim and tear at its skin and flesh.

▲ Deinonychus

34 Deinonychus also had a huge hooked claw, as big as your hand, on the second toe of each foot. This claw could kick out and flick down like a pointed knife to slash pieces out of the prey.

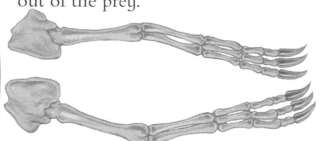

35 Baryonyx also had a large claw but this was on the thumb of each hand. It may have worked as a fish-hook to snatch fish from water. This is another clue that Baryonyx probably ate fish.

◄ These giant arms of the dinosaur Deinocheirus were found in Mongolia. Each one was bigger than a human, but nothing else of the skeleton has yet been found.

36
Iguanodon had claws on its feet. But these were rounded and blunt and looked more like hooves.

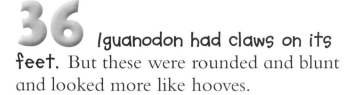

QUIZ 2

Compare these modern animals' claws to the dinosaurs and their claws shown here. Which modern animal has claws with a similar shape and job to each dinosaur?

1. Lion – sharp, tearing claws
2. Deer – Rounded blunt hooves
3. Elephant – Flat, nail–like claws
4. Mole – Broad, strong digging claws

1. Deinonychus 2. Iguanodon 3. Apatosaurus 4. Hypsilophodon

37
Iguanodon also had stubby claws on its hands. However its thumb claw was longer and shaped like a spike, perhaps for stabbing enemies.

38
Giant sauropod dinosaurs had almost flat claws. Dinosaurs like Apatosaurus looked like they had toenails on their huge feet!

Deadly meat-eaters

39 The biggest meat-eating dinosaurs were the largest predators (hunters) ever to walk the Earth. Different types came and went during the Age of Dinosaurs. Allosaurus was from the middle of this time span. One of the last dinosaurs was also one of the largest predators - Tyrannosaurus. An earlier hunting dinosaur from South America was even more huge - Giganotosaurus.

I DON'T BELIEVE IT!

Some meat-eating dinosaurs not only bit their prey, but also each other! Fossils of several Tyrannosaurus had bite marks on the head. Perhaps they fought each other to become chief in the group, like wolves today.

40 **These great predators were well equipped for hunting large prey — including other dinosaurs.** They all had massive mouths armed with long sharp teeth in powerful jaws. They had long, strong back legs for fast running, and enormous toe claws for kicking and holding down victims.

41 **Meat-eating dinosaurs probably caught their food in various ways.** They might lurk behind rocks or trees and rush out to surprise a victim. They might race as fast as possible after prey which ran away. They might plod steadily for a great time to tire out their meal. They might even scavenge - feast on the bodies of creatures which were dead or dying from old age or injury.

Albertosaurus was from North America. It was 9 metres long and weighed 1 tonne.

Allosaurus was 11 metres long and weighed 2 tonnes. It came from North America.

Carnotaurus from South America was 7.5 metres long and weighed 1 tonne

The famous Tyrannosaurus rex was 13 metres long and weighed 6 tonnes. It lived in North America.

Spinosaurus came from Africa. It was 14 metres long and weighed 4 tonnes.

The biggest carnivore was Giganotosaurus. It was a massive 15 metres long and weighed 7 tonnes!

Look! Listen! Sniff!

42 **Like the reptiles of today, dinosaurs could see, hear and smell the world around them.** We know this from fossils. The preserved fossil skulls had spaces for eyes, ears and nostrils.

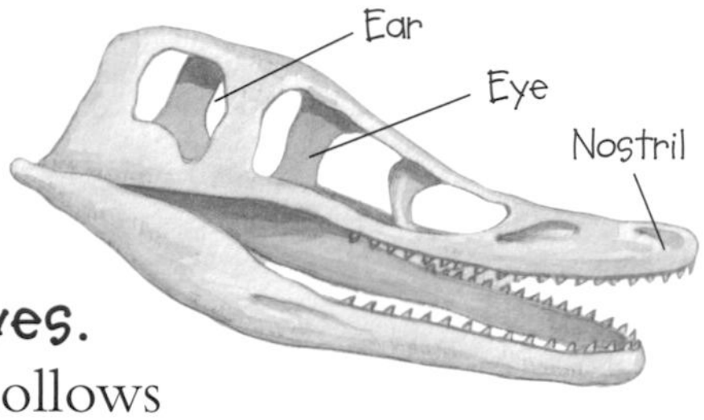

Ear

Eye

Nostril

43 **Some dinosaurs like Troodon had very big eyes.** There are large, bowl-shaped hollows in the fossil skull for them. Today's animals with big eyes can see well in the dark, like mice, owls and night-time lizards. Perhaps Troodon prowled through the forest at night, peering in the gloom for small creatures to eat.

44 **There are also spaces on the sides of the head where Troodon had its ears.** Dinosaur ears were round and flat, like the ears of other reptiles. Troodon could hear the tiny noises of little animals moving about in the dark.

◀ Troodon was about 2 metres long and lived in North America 70 million years ago. You can see here the large eye sockets.

45 The nostrils of Troodon, where it breathed in air and smelled scents, were two holes at the front of its snout. With its delicate sense of smell, Troodon could sniff out its prey of insects, worms, little reptiles such as lizards, and small shrew-like mammals.

▲ Corythosaurus has a bony plate on its head, instead of the tube like Parasaurolophus.

46 Dinosaurs used their eyes, ears and noses not only to find food, but also to detect enemies – and each other. Parasaurolophus had a long, hollow, tube-like crest on its head. Perhaps it blew air along this to make a noise like a trumpet, as an elephant does today with its trunk.

▶ Parasaurolophus was a 'duck–billed' dinosaur or hadrosaur. It was about 10 metres long and lived 80 million years ago in North America.

BIGGER EYES, BETTER SIGHT

Make a Troodon mask from card. Carefully cut out the shape as shown. Carefully cut out two small eye holes, each just 1cm across. Attach elastic so you can wear the mask and find out how little you can see. Carefully make the eye holes as large as the eyes of the real Troodon. Now you can have a much bigger, clearer view of the world!

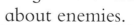

47 Dinosaurs like Parasaurolophus may have made noises to send messages to other members of their group or herd. Different messages could tell the others about finding food or warn them about enemies.

Living with dinosaurs

48 **All dinosaurs walked and ran on land, as far as we know.** No dinosaurs could fly in the air or spend their lives swimming in the water. But many other creatures, which lived at the same time as the dinosaurs, could fly or swim. Some were reptiles, like the dinosaurs.

49 **Ichthyosaurs were reptiles that lived in the sea.** They were shaped like dolphins, long and slim with fins and a tail. They chased after fish to eat.

50 **Plesiosaurs were also reptiles that swam in the sea.** They had long necks, tubby bodies, four large flippers and a short tail.

Predators like Velociraptor were meat-eating dinosaurs with large arms, wrists and hands. Over millions of years these could have evolved feathers to become a bird's wings.

51 **Turtles were another kind of reptile that swam in the sea during the Age of Dinosaurs.** Each had a strong, domed shell and four flippers. Turtles still survive today, but ichthyosaurs and plesiosaurs died out with the dinosaurs, long ago.

Turtle

Plesiosaur

Ichthyosaur

Hadrosaurs like Anatosaurus were duck-billed dinosaurs with a tall, deep tail like a crocodile's tail. Perhaps Anatosaurus swished this from side to side to swim now and again. But it did not live in the water.

53 **Birds first appeared about 150 million years ago.** It is possible that over millions of years certain small, meat-eating dinosaurs called raptors developed feathers. Slowly their arms became wings. Gradually they evolved into the very first birds.

54 **Birds evolved after the dinosaurs, but birds did overlap with the dinosaurs.** Some dived for fish in the sea, very much like birds such as gulls and terns today.

Ichthyornis

52 **Pterosaurs were reptiles that could fly.** They had thin, skin-like wings held out by long finger bones. Some soared over the sea and grabbed small fish in their sharp-toothed, beak-shaped mouths. Others swooped on small land animals.

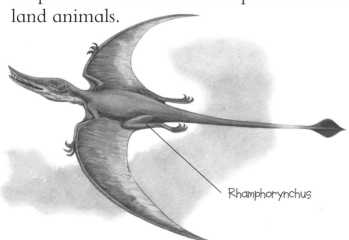

Rhamphorynchus

QUIZ

Which of these are
NOT dinosaurs?

A Pterosaur

B Raptor

C Plesiosaur

D Hadrosaur

E Ichthyosaur

F Bird

A Pterosaur, C Plesiosaur,
E Ichthyosaur, F Bird

Fastest and slowest

55 Dinosaurs walked and ran at different speeds, according to their size and shape. In the world today, cheetahs and ostriches are slim with long legs and run very fast. Elephants and hippos are massive heavyweights and plod slowly. Dinosaurs were similar. Some were big, heavy and slow. Others were slim, light and speedy.

▲ Struthiomimus lived about 75 million years ago in north-west North America.

56 Struthiomimus was one of the fastest of all the dinosaurs. It was more than 2 metres tall and 4 metres long. It had very long back legs and large clawed feet, like an ostrich. It also had a horny beak-shaped mouth for pecking food, like an ostrich. This is why it is also called an 'ostrich-dinosaur'. It could probably run at more than 70 kilometres per hour.

▼ Coelophysis was 3 metres long. It was one of the earliest dinosaurs, living about 220 million years ago.

57 Muttaburrasaurus was a huge ornithopod type of dinosaur, a cousin of *Iguanodon*. It probably walked about as fast as you, around 4-5 kilometres per hour. It might have been able to gallop along at a top speed of 15 kilometres per hour, making the ground shake with its 4-tonne weight!

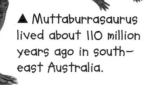

▲ Muttaburrasaurus lived about 110 million years ago in south-east Australia.

58 Coelophysis was a slim, lightweight dinosaur. It could probably trot, jump, leap and dart about with great agility. Sometimes it ran upright on its two back legs. Or it could bound along on all fours like a dog at more than 30 kilometres per hour.

QUIZ 4

Put these dinosaurs and today's animals in order of top running speed, from slowest to fastest.

Human (40 km/h)

Cheetah (100–plus km/h)

Struthiomimus (70 km/h)

Muttaburrasaurus (15 km/h)

Sloth (0.2 km/h)

Coelophysis (30 km/h)

Sloth, Muttaburrasaurus, Coelophysis, Human, Struthiomimus, Cheetah

Dinosaur tanks

59 Some dinosaurs had body defences against predators. These might be large horns and spikes, or thick hard lumps of bone like armour-plating. Most armoured dinosaurs were plant-eaters. They had to defend themselves against big meat-eating dinosaurs such as Tyrannosaurus.

60 Triceratops had three horns, one on its nose and two much longer ones above its eyes. It also has a wide shield-like piece of bone over its neck and shoulders. The horns and neck frill made Triceratops look very fearsome. But most of the time it quietly ate plants. If it was attacked, Triceratops could charge at the enemy and jab with its horns, like a rhino does today.

Triceratops was 9 metres long and weighed over 5 tonnes. It lived 65 million years ago in North America.

61 **Euoplocephalus was a well–armoured dinosaur.** It had bands of thick, leathery skin across its back. Big, hard, pointed lumps of bone were set into this skin like studs on a leather belt. Euoplocephalus also had a great lump of bone on its tail. It measured almost one metre across and looked like a massive hammer or club. Euoplocephalus could swing it at predators to injure them or break their legs.

DESIGN A DINOSAUR!

Make an imaginary dinosaur! It might have the body armour and tail club of Euoplocephalus, or the head horns and neck frill of Triceratops.
You can draw your dinosaur, or make it out of pieces of card or from modelling clay. You can give it a made-up name, like Euoplo-ceratops or Tri-cephalus.
How well protected is your dinosaur? How does it compare to some well-armoured creatures of today, such as a tortoise, armadillo or porcupine?

Styracosaurus

Protoceratops

Euoplocephalus

Dinosaur eggs and nests

62 Like most reptiles today, dinosaurs produced young by laying eggs. These hatched out into baby dinosaurs which gradually grew into adults.

▲ A fossilised baby developing inside an egg.

Fossils have been found of eggs with dinosaurs still developing inside, as well as fossils of just-hatched baby dinosaurs.

63 Many kinds of dinosaur eggs have been found. Protoceratops was a pig-sized dinosaur that lived 85 million years ago in what is now the Gobi Desert of Asia.

▲ Protoceratops egg

64 A Protoceratops female arranged her eggs. The eggs were carefully positioned in a spiral shape, or in circles one within the other.

▼ A female Protoceratops with her eggs

65 Protoceratops scraped a bowl-shaped nest about one metre across in the dry soil. Probably the female did this. Today, only female reptiles make nests and some care for the eggs or babies. Male reptiles take no part.

▲ Hadrosaur egg

66 The eggs probably hatched after a few weeks. The eggshell was slightly leathery and bendy, like most reptile eggshells today, and not brittle or hard like a bird's.

67 Fossils of baby Protoceratops show that they looked very much like their parents. But the neck frill of the baby Protoceratops was not as large compared to the rest of the body, as in the adult. As the youngster grew, the frill grew faster than the rest of the body. In humans, a baby's head is larger compared to the rest of its body. As the baby's body grows, its head grows slower.

▶ This is part of a life-size Tyrannosaurus egg.

QUIZ 5

1. How long was Triceratops?
2. How many horns did Triceratops have?
3. How many eggs did a female Protoceratops lay?
4. Did dinosaurs lay hard eggs like birds, or bendy eggs?
5. How long was a Tyrannosaurus rex egg?

1. 9 metres 2. Three 3. About 20 eggs 4. They laid bendy, leathery eggs 5. 40 centimetres

68 Other dinosaurs laid different sizes and shapes of eggs. Huge sauropod dinosaurs like Brachiosaurus probably laid rounded eggs as big as basketballs. Eggs of big meat-eaters like Tyrannosaurus were more sausage-shaped, 40 centimetres long and 15 centimetres wide.

69 Most dinosaurs simply laid their eggs in a nest or buried in soil, and left them to hatch on their own. The baby dinosaurs had to find their own food and defend themselves against enemies. But other dinosaurs looked after their babies.

Dinosaur babies

70 Some dinosaur parents looked after their babies and even brought them food in the nest. Fossils of the hadrosaur dinosaur Maiasaura included nests, eggs, babies after hatching, and broken eggshells. Some fossils were of unhatched eggs but broken into many small parts, as though squashed by the babies which had already come out of their eggs.

71 The newly-hatched Maiasaura babies had to stay in the nest. They could not run away because their leg bones had not yet become strong and hard. The nest was a mound of mud about 2 metres across, and up to 20 babies lived in it.

A full-grown Maiasaura was about 9 metres long and weighed around 3 tonnes. A newly-hatched Maiasaura baby was only 30–40 centimetres long. Maiasaura lived about 75 million years ago in North America.

Hundreds of fossil Maiasaura nests have been found close together, showing that these dinosaurs bred in groups or colonies. The nests showed signs of being dug out and repaired year after year, which suggests the dinosaurs kept coming back to the same place to breed.

72 Fossils of Maiasaura nests also contain fossilised twigs, berries and other bits of plants. Maiasaura was a plant-eating dinosaur, and it seems that one or both parents brought food to the nest for their babies to eat. The tiny teeth of the babies already had slight scratches and other marks where they had been worn while eating food. This supports the idea that parent Maiasaura brought food to their babies in the nest.

The end for the dinosaurs

73 **All dinosaurs on Earth died out by 65 million years ago.** There are dinosaur fossils in the rocks up to this time, but there are none after. There are, though, fossils of other creatures like fish, insects, birds and mammals. What happened to wipe out some of the biggest, most numerous and most successful animals the world has ever seen? There are many ideas. It could have been one disaster, or a combination of several.

74 **The dinosaurs may have been killed by a giant lump of rock, a meteorite.** This may have come from outer space and smashed into the Earth. It threw up vast clouds of water, rocks, ash and dust that blotted out the sun for many years. Plants could not grow in the gloom so plant-eating dinosaurs died out. Meat-eating dinosaurs had no food so they died as well.

77 It might be that dinosaur eggs were eaten by a plague of animals. Small, shrew-like mammals were around at the time. They may have eaten the eggs at night as the dinosaurs slept.

75 Many volcanoes around the Earth could have erupted all at the same time. This would have thrown out red-hot rocks, ash, dust and clouds of poison gas. Dinosaurs would have choked and died in the gloom.

76 Dinosaurs might have been killed by a disease. This could have gradually spread among all the dinosaurs and killed them off.

METEORITE SMASH!

You will need:

a plastic bowl   a place where a
cooking flour   mess does not
a large pebble   matter!
a desk light

Ask an adult for help. Put the flour in the bowl. This is Earth's surface. Place the desk light so it shines over the top of the bowl. This is the sun. The pebble is the meteorite from space. WHAM! Drop the pebble into the bowl. See how the tiny bits of flour float in the air like a mist, making the 'sun' dimmer. A real meteorite smash may have been the beginning of the end for the dinosaurs.

After the dinosaurs

78 From 65 million years ago there were no dinosaurs left.
Dinosaurs were not the only group of animals to perish at that time. The flying reptiles called pterosaurs, the swimming reptiles, ichthyosaurs and plesiosaurs, also died. When a group of living things dies out completely, this is known as extinction. When many groups of living things all disappear at about the same time, this is a mass extinction.

◄ Diatryma, a giant flightless bird

79 Even though many kinds of animals and plants died out 65 million years ago, many other groups lived on. Insects, worms, fish, birds and mammals all survived the mass extinction – and these groups are still alive today.

80 Even though the dinosaurs and many other reptiles died out in the mass extinction, several other groups of reptiles did not. Crocodiles, turtles and tortoises, lizards and snakes all survived. Why some kinds of reptiles like dinosaurs died out in the mass extinction, yet other types did not still puzzles dinosaur experts today.

▼ The mass extinction of 65 million years ago killed the dinosaurs and many other kinds of animals and plants. But plenty of living things survived, as shown here.

▼ Hesperocyon   ▼ Hyracotherium

81 After the mass extinction, two main groups of animals began to take the place of the dinosaurs and spread over the land. These were birds and mammals. No longer were mammals small and skulking, coming out only after dark when the dinosaurs were asleep. The mammals changed or evolved to become bigger, with many kinds from peaceful plant-eaters to huge, fierce predators.

I DON'T BELIEVE IT!

The earliest birds had wings and flapped through the skies. But many of the birds which appeared after the dinosaurs could not fly!

Myths and mistakes

82 As far as we can tell from the clues we have, some of the ideas which have grown up about dinosaurs are not true. For example, dinosaurs are shown in different colours such as brown or green. Some have patches or stripes. But no one knows the true colours of dinosaurs. There are a few fossils of dinosaur skin. But being fossils, these have turned to stone and so they are the colour of stone. They are no longer the colour of the original dinosaur skin.

◄ We really have no idea what colour the dinosaurs were. We can guess by looking at reptiles today, but they could have been any colour!

◄ This is a fossil of the skin of Edmontosaurus. You can see the texture of the skin, but the only colour is of the rock.

83 Similarly, for many years people thought that all dinosaurs were slow and stupid animals. But they were not. Some dinosaurs were quick and agile. Also some, like Troodon, had big brains for their body size. They may have been quite 'clever'.

▲ Troodon had a large brain for its body size, almost the same as a monkey of today.

84

Scientists began to study fossils of dinosaurs about 160 years ago, in the 19th century. These first dinosaurs to be studied were very big, such as Megalosaurus, Iguanodon and Plateosaurus. So the idea grew up that all dinosaurs were huge. But they were not. Compsognathus, one of the smallest dinosaurs, was only 75 centimetres long – about as big as a pet cat of today.

◄ Compsognathus weighed only 3 kilograms and lived 155 million years ago in Europe.

◄ Its name means 'elegant jaw'. Its teeth were small and spaced apart from each other. This makes it likely that Compsognathus ate small reptiles and insects, rather than attacking large prey.

▲ These Wannanosaurus are using their bony skull caps to fight over territory, food or a mate. The battle is fierce, but Wannanosaurus was only about 60 centimetres long! It lived in Asia about 85 million years ago.

I DON'T BELIEVE IT!

One dinosaur's thumb was put on its nose! When scientists first dug up fossils of Iguanodon, they found a bone shaped like a horn, as if for Iguanodon's nose. Most scientists now believe that the spike was a thumb–claw.

85

Another idea grew up that early cave–people had to fight against dinosaurs and kill them – or the other way around. But they did not. There was a very long gap, more than 60 million years, between the very last of the dinosaurs and the earliest people.

86

Some people believe that dinosaurs may survive today in remote, faraway places on Earth, such as thick jungle or ocean islands. But most of the Earth has now been visited and explored, and no living dinosaurs have been seen.

How do we know?

87 **We know about dinosaurs mainly from their fossils.** Fossils took thousands or millions of years to form. Most fossils form on the bottoms of lakes, rivers or seas, where sand and mud can quickly cover them over and begin to preserve them. If the animal is on dry land, they are more likely to be eaten, or simply to rot away to nothing.

Fossils take millions of years to form. Firstly, an animal, like this trilobite dies. Trilobites lived in the sea about 600 million years ago, long before the first dinosaurs.

▼ Stegoceras was a pachycephalosaur or 'bone–head' dinosaur. It had a very thick layer of bone on top of its head, like an armoured helmet. Its name means 'horny roof'!

Stegoceras was 2 metres long. We can tell from its teeth that it was a herbivore, or plant–eater. We can tell roughly the date of the rocks in which the fossil was preserved, so can tell that it lived 70 million years ago on the west coast of what is now North America. Like many plant–eaters, it probably lived in a large herd.

88 **The body parts most likely to fossilize were the hardest ones, which rot away most slowly after death.** These included animal parts such as bones, teeth, horns, claws and shells, and plant parts such as bark, seeds and cones.

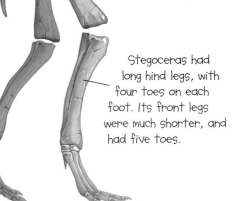

Stegoceras had long hind legs, with four toes on each foot. Its front legs were much shorter, and had five toes.

89 **Very rarely, a dinosaur or other living thing was buried soon after it died.** Then a few of the softer body parts also became fossils, such as bits of skin or the remains of the last meal in the stomach.

The soft parts rot away.

The remaining shell is buried in mud.

The mud turns to rock, which turns the shell to rock, and makes a fossil.

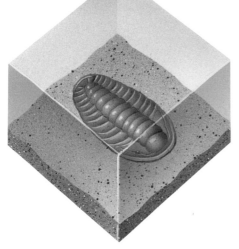

The skull of Stegoceras was dome-shaped. The thickest part of the bony plate was 6 centimetres thick, and it protected the brain. From this scientists have guessed that Stegoceras may have had head-butting contents.

▼ Stegoceras may have had head-butting contests with rivals at breeding time, like male sheep and goats do today.

91 Dinosaur droppings also formed fossils! They have broken bits of food inside, showing what the dinosaur ate. Some dinosaur droppings are as big as a TV set!

90 Not all dinosaur fossils are from the actual bodies of dinosaurs. Some are the signs, traces or remains which they left while alive. These include eggshells, nests, tunnels, footprints, and claw and teeth marks on food.

QUIZ 6

What formed fossils?

Which body parts of a dinosaur were most likely to become fossils? Remember, fossils form from the hardest, toughest bits that last long enough to become buried in the rocks and turned to stone.

Skull bone	Blood
Muscle	Claws
Leg bone	Eye
Scaly skin	Teeth

Skull bone, leg bone, teeth, claws are most likely to form fossils

Digging up dinosaurs

92 Every year, thousands of dinosaur fossils are discovered. Most of them are from dinosaurs already known to scientists. But five or ten might be from new kinds of dinosaurs. From the fossils, scientists try to work out what the dinosaur looked like and how it lived, all those millions of years ago.

▼ These are paleontologists, scientists that look for and study dinosaur bones, uncovering a new skeleton.

93 Most dinosaur fossils are found by hard work. Fossil experts called paleontologists study the rocks in a region and decide where fossils are most likely to occur. They spend weeks chipping and digging the rock. They look closely at every tiny piece to see if it is part of a fossil. However some dinosaur fossils are found by luck. People out walking in the countryside come across a fossil tooth or bone by chance. What a discovery!

94 Finding all the fossils of a single dinosaur, neatly in position as in life, is very rare indeed. Usually only a few fossil parts are found from each dinosaur. These are nearly always jumbled up and broken.

People dig carefully into the rock with hammers, picks and brushes.

Scientists make notes, sketches and photographs, to record every stage of the fossil 'dig'.

95

The fossils are taken back to the paleontology laboratory. They are cleaned and laid out to see which parts are which. It is like trying to put together a jigsaw, with most of the pieces missing. Even those which remain are bent and torn. The fossils are put back together, then soft body parts which did not form fossils, such as skin, are added. Scientists use clues from similar animals alive today, such as crocodiles, to help 'rebuild' the dinosaur.

▲ cleaning fossils

▲ laying out fossils

▲ Finally, the rebuilt skeleton is displayed in a museum.

Fossils are solid rock and very heavy, but also brittle and easy to crack. So they may need to be wrapped in a strong casing such as plaster-of-paris or glass-fibre.

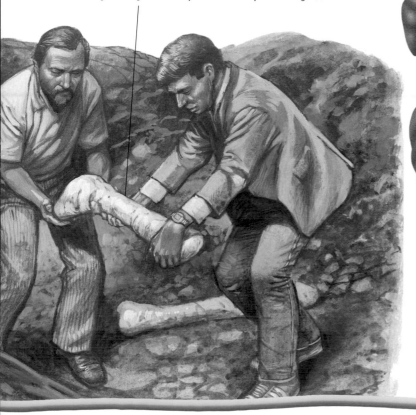

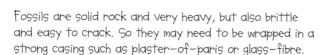

QUIZ 7

1. What do we call a scientist that studies fossils?

2. How is a fossil 'dig' recorded?

3. How are fossils packed to protect them?

4. What animals can scientists compare dinosaurs fossils with?

1. A Paleontologist 2. Notes, sketches and photographs 3. They are put in plaster-of-paris or glass-fibre 4. Crocodiles

Finding new dinosaurs

96 The first fossils of dinosaurs to be studied by scientists came from Europe and North America. However since those early discoveries, in the 1830s and 1840s, dinosaur fossils have been found all over the world.

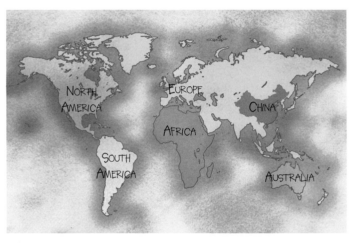

97 Some of the most exciting fossils from recent years are being found in China. They include Caudipteryx, Protoarchaeopteryx and Sinosauropteryx. Tiny details of the fossils show that these strange creatures may have had feathers. Today, any creature with feathers is a bird. So were they birds? Or were they dinosaurs with feathers? Nobody knows yet!

Sinosauropteryx

Caudipteryx

Protoarchaeopteryx

98 Many more exciting finds are being made in Australia, Africa and South America. The small plant-eater Leaellynasaura, about 2 metres long and 1 metre tall, lived in Australia 110 million years ago. It may have slept through a cold, snowy winter. Fossils of giant sauropod dinosaurs such as Jobaria and Janenschia have been uncovered in Africa. In South America there are fossil finds of the biggest plant-eaters and meat-eaters, such as Argentinosaurus and Giganotosaurus.

► Jobaria and Janenschia are two newly discovered, giant sauropod dinosaurs from Africa

99 Some people believe that one day, dinosaurs may be brought back to life. This has already happened but only in stories, such as the Jurassic Park films. However scientists are trying to obtain genetic material, the chemical called DNA, from fossils. The genetic material may contain the 'instructions' for how a dinosaur grew and lived.

100 Dinosaurs lived and died long, long ago. Their world has been and gone, and cannot alter. But what is changing is our knowledge of the dinosaurs. Every year we know more about them. One sure thing about dinosaurs is that what we know now, will change in the future.

▲ Leaellynasaura was discovered in 1989, in a place called 'Dinosaur Cove' near Melbourne, Australia. The scientists were Pat and Thomas Rich who found its fossils.

I DON'T BELIEVE IT!

One dinosaur is named after a young girl! Leaellynasaura was named after the daughter of the scientists who found its fossils!

Index